Landscape by Design

Perimeter and Area

Christine Dugan

Consultants

Pamela Dase, M.A.Ed.
National Board Certified Teacher

Barbara Talley, M.S.
Texas A&M University

Publishing Credits

Dona Herweck Rice, *Editor-in-Chief*
Robin Erickson, *Production Director*
Lee Aucoin, *Creative Director*
Timothy J. Bradley, *Illustration Manager*
Sara Johnson, M.S.Ed., *Senior Editor*
Aubrie Nielsen, M.S.Ed., *Associate Education Editor*
Jennifer Kim, M.A.Ed., *Associate Education Editor*
Neri Garcia, *Senior Designer*
Stephanie Reid, *Photo Editor*
Rachelle Cracchiolo, M.S.Ed., *Publisher*

Image Credits

Cover Peter Graham/Shutterstock, p.1 Peter Graham/Shutterstock, p.4 Howard Sandler/Shutterstock; p.5 Scott E. Feuer/Shutterstock; p.6 Scott E. Feuer/Shutterstock; p.7 Getty Images/Comstock Images; p.7 (inset) Romvo/Shutterstock; p.8 (top) Vladimir Korostyshevskiy/Shutterstock; p.8 (bottom) JPagetRFphotos/Shutterstock; p.10 (left) Gualberto Becerra/Shutterstock; p.10 (right) Philip Date/Shutterstock; p.11 Chrislofoto/Shutterstock; p.12 (left) charles taylor/Shutterstock; p.12 (right) Peter Graham/Shutterstock; p.13 Leigh Clapp/Getty Images; p.14 Zocchi/Shutterstock; p.14 (inset) Photosindiacom, LLC/Shutterstock; p.15 (top) Pooh/Shutterstock; p.15 (bottom) Zocchi/Shutterstock; p.16 Mark Winfrey/Shutterstock; p.17 EuToch/Shutterstock; p.18 (top) Scott E. Feuer/Shutterstock; p.18 (bottom) charobnica/Shutterstock; p.19 Scott E. Feuer/Shutterstock; p.20 (left) Gelpi/Shutterstock; p.20 (center) Orange Line Media/Shutterstock; p.20 (right) Bruce Works/Shutterstock; p.20 (top) Yurchyks/Shutterstock; p.21 (left) Sever180/Shutterstock, (right) Romvo/Shutterstock; p.22 Pack-Shot/Shutterstock; p.23 (top) Tratong/Shutterstock, (back) Jennifer Stone/Shutterstock; p.24 (top) Pack-Shot/Shutterstock; p.24 (bottom) M. Moita/Shutterstock; p.25 Moth/Dreamstime; p.26 Getty Images/Images Bazaar; p.27 (top) Andrey.tiyk/Shutterstock; p.27 (bottom) Anton Balazh/Shutterstock; p.27 (right) Fotokostic/Shutterstock; p.28 Suzanne Tucker/Shutterstock; All other images: Shutterstock

---

Teacher Created Materials

5301 Oceanus Drive
Huntington Beach, CA 92649-1030
http://www.tcmpub.com
ISBN 978-1-4333-3459-7
© 2012 Teacher Created Materials, Inc.

Table of Contents

Designing Our Yard

Today is an exciting day! My family is getting ready to design our backyard. We moved into our house a few years ago. Since then, we have done a lot of work to the inside of the house. We painted, bought new furniture, and decorated. Now it's time to focus on getting our yard in order. I love the outdoors, so I can't wait!

Job Requirements

A landscape designer must be able to organize outdoor spaces. But the job also requires knowing a lot about plants, including being able to pick the right trees, shrubs, bushes, and flowers for the climate.

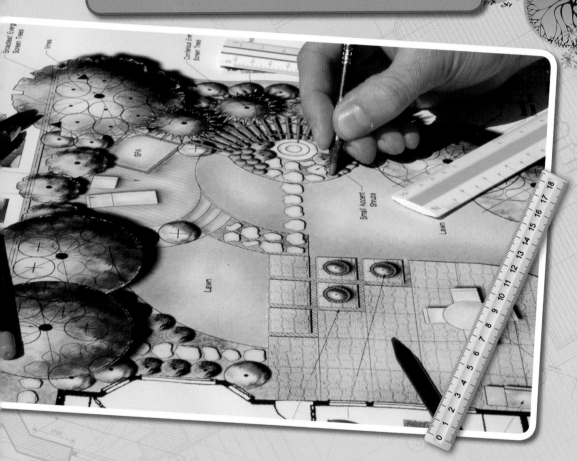

I think that planning an outdoor space takes a lot of creativity. We know there are many ways to design the backyard. My parents hired a landscape designer. That is someone who plans and designs outdoor spaces. A landscape designer has to choose the kind of yard that fits with a house or building. The indoor and outdoor spaces should work well together.

Landscape designers need strong math skills to do their jobs. Just as architects (AHR-ki-tekts) plan structures and indoor spaces, landscape designers need to fit things together in the yard. They must use **area** and **perimeter** (puh-RIM-i-ter) to measure spaces of different shapes.

A yard usually includes many elements, such as plants, rocks and stones, and furniture. Our landscape designer has to be able to fit everything we want in the space we have. My dad wants a lawn and a **patio**. My mom wants a garden and a lot of plants. My brother and I want a swimming pool. My family wonders how all of that will look together.

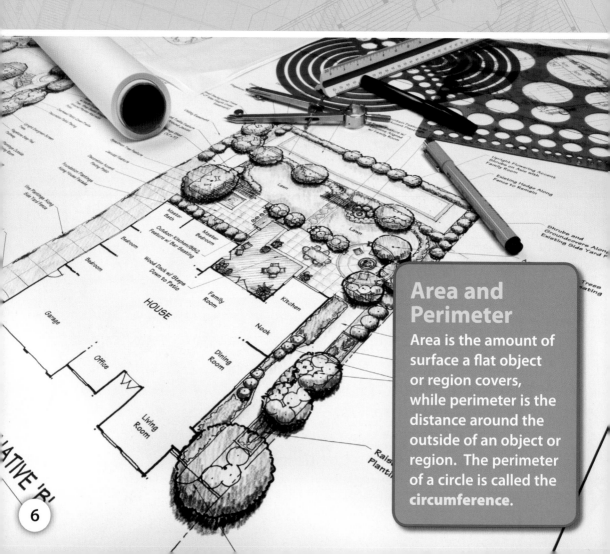

Area and Perimeter

Area is the amount of surface a flat object or region covers, while perimeter is the distance around the outside of an object or region. The perimeter of a circle is called the **circumference**.

First, we meet with our designer to brainstorm ideas. Our designer starts by talking about the shape of our lawn. He says that the shape of the lawn is an important decision. It can determine where other things are placed in the backyard.

Measuring the Lawn

My dad thinks that our lawn should be the central part of our yard. A lawn can be used for many different things. Dad hopes that we can play all sorts of games on the grass. We can spread out blankets and have picnics on our new lawn. Our dog will also enjoy having a soft and comfortable place to nap in the sun.

Spectacular Design

The gardens of the palace of Versailles (ver-SAHY) in France are some of the most famous gardens in the world. They cover almost 5,000 miles (8,047 km). That's a lot of lawn to mow!

Once we decide on the size of our lawn, our landscape designer needs to measure the space. He has to know how much seed to buy when he plants the grass. He has to carefully measure each side of the shape to determine the area and perimeter. Knowing the distance around the outside of the lawn helps our designer decide how many plants are needed to **border** it.

LET'S EXPLORE MATH

This lawn is a **trapezoid**. A trapezoid is a **polygon**. It has two parallel sides, called bases (b_1 and b_2), and two sides connecting them. The height (h) of the trapezoid describes how tall it is and may not be one of the sides.

The perimeter of any polygon is the sum of the lengths of its sides.

The area of a trapezoid is found with the **formula** $A = \frac{1}{2}(b_1 + b_2)h$.

What are the perimeter and area of the lawn below?

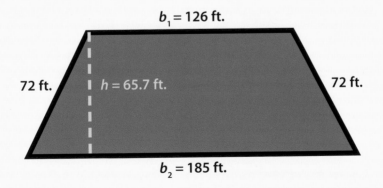

$b_1 = 126$ ft.

72 ft. $h = 65.7$ ft.   72 ft.

$b_2 = 185$ ft.

Planning for a Patio

We are very lucky to live in a place that has a mild **climate**, which means it is never too cold or too hot. My parents hope we can use our backyard all year long. They want to start preparing and eating meals outside. In order to do this, we need a space in our backyard for a table and chairs. My dad also wants to use his barbecue grill more. We need a patio!

LET'S EXPLORE MATH

Some people may design a patio using stones in the shape of hexagons. In a regular hexagon, all the sides are the same length.

What is the perimeter of this regular hexagon?

5.1 in.

My parents discuss how to build a patio with our landscape designer. They must decide what kind of material to use for the patio surface. There are a lot of choices, from bricks to large stones, from concrete to gravel. They decide on a solid, level surface. That way, the table and chair legs will stay even and flat. They choose brick for our patio.

Different Kinds of Gardens

My dad is most interested in the design of the lawn and the patio. My mom is most excited about planting a garden.

Our landscape designer wants to help plan the garden. He is excited that our family is interested in growing healthy fruits and vegetables. But first he wants to talk about making room for a rock garden. He thinks a circular rock garden will be **unique** (yoo-NEEK).

Backyard Circles

Circles are often used in outdoor spaces. A small **gazebo**, for example, is a circular building that is often found in parks. Birdbaths, flower pots, and fire pits are often round as well.

Our designer shows us a sketch. The rock garden will look really interesting. It will be in a shady corner of the yard where it is hard to grow things. Our designer tells us that mixing shapes is a good way to blend the elements of our yard. Placing a round rock garden next to a space shaped like a rectangle or octagon is an attractive **contrast**.

Pi

Pi (PAHY) is a constant in math whose value is the ratio of the circumference of any circle to the diameter. Since pi is an **irrational number**, it cannot be expressed exactly as a fraction or decimal. Mathematicians use the approximations $\frac{22}{7}$ and 3.14 for pi. It is represented by the symbol π.

LET'S EXPLORE MATH

Look at the formulas below for the area and circumference of a circle. The *d* represents the **diameter**, and the *r* represents the **radius**.

Circumference of a circle: $C = \pi d$ or $C = 2\pi r$

Area of a circle: $A = \pi r^2$

Use $\frac{22}{7}$ or 3.14 as the value of π.

2.4m

a. What is the circumference of this circle? Round your answer to the nearest hundredth. Why might you need to know the circumference of a circle in a garden?

b. What is the area of this circle? Round your answer to the nearest hundredth. Why might you need to know the area of a circle in a garden?

Planting Food

After the rock garden is discussed, we talk about planting a fruit and vegetable garden. My mom has many ideas about the kinds of foods she wants to grow. We have to learn which types of crops will grow well in our town's climate. Then we have to work with the designer to plan our planting area.

The garden is going to be shaped like a rectangle. Our designer tells us to think about spacing our plants by dividing the rectangle into smaller triangles. We must think about how much room the plants will need to grow. We have a lot of planning to do!

Organic Gardening

Gardens require a lot of work. You have to keep weeds and pests out of your garden. Many people practice organic gardening. This means they don't use pesticides or other kinds of chemicals to help the plants grow and stay healthy.

Growing crops can be challenging in colder climates. Gardeners in these regions plant vegetables in a cold frame or greenhouse to protect them from the harsh weather.

LET'S EXPLORE MATH

To find the area of a triangle, you will need to use the formula: $A = \frac{1}{2}(bh)$. The height (h) of the triangle describes how tall the triangle is. The height is always **perpendicular** (pur-puhn-DIK-yuh-ler) to the base (b).

a. Find the perimeter and area of the triangle below.

b. Why is the height not included when measuring the perimeter of this triangle?

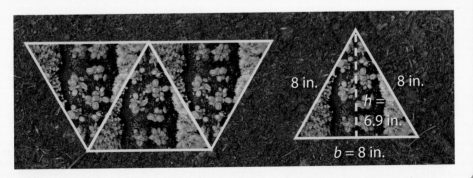

8 in.   8 in.

$h = 6.9$ in.

$b = 8$ in.

A New Swimming Pool

It has been interesting to talk about patios, gardens, and lawns. But I am finally ready to hear more about the most exciting part of our yard—the swimming pool! My brother and I have been dreaming of having our own pool since we were young. I am looking forward to having my friends over to swim. I know that our family will really enjoy having this pool in the hot summertime.

Safety First

People who have pools in their backyards often put locked gates around them. That way, young children or others who cannot swim will not wander into the water and possibly drown.

Our landscape designer has to work with other professionals who know how to build pools. Right now, he is interested in how much space the pool will take up in the yard. He needs to know the area and perimeter of the pool to know how it will fit with other things in the yard.

Pools come in all shapes and sizes. Our family decides on a shape that is an **irregular** polygon. The lengths of the sides and the measure of the **angles** are not all the same in an irregular polygon.

Some pools are not polygons at all. This pool has no straight sides.

LET'S EXPLORE MATH

Look at the sketch of the swimming pool that the family chose for their yard. It is an irregular polygon.

You can find the area of an irregular polygon by dividing it into regular polygons. Divide this quadrilateral into a triangle and a trapezoid and find their areas. Then find the area of the whole figure.

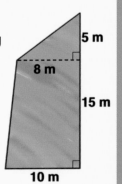

5 m

8 m

15 m

10 m

a. What is the area of the triangle?

b. What is the area of the trapezoid?

c. Find the sum of the two areas to determine the area of the swimming pool.

Understanding Angles

Now that we have decided on different parts of the yard, our designer needs to give us some updated plans. We have made a lot of decisions. But how will our ideas look when the work is finished?

Our landscape designer provides drawn and labeled plans that show exactly what our yard will look like. These plans are more detailed and accurate than a sketch. They include shapes and angles of all kinds. Everything is drawn very carefully.

Our designer offered several possible designs for our yard.

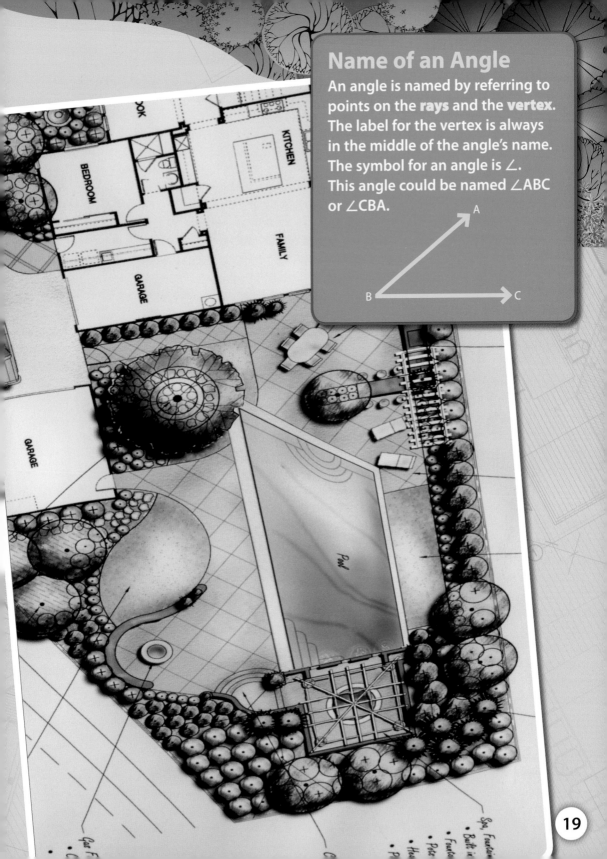

Name of an Angle

An angle is named by referring to points on the **rays** and the **vertex**. The label for the vertex is always in the middle of the angle's name. The symbol for an angle is ∠. This angle could be named ∠ABC or ∠CBA.

The plans show our backyard drawn to **scale**. This means all parts of the drawing are shown in relation to the size of actual objects. The landscape designer also has to use different tools, such as a **protractor** (proh-TRAK-ter), to measure the angles of various shapes.

Angle Measures

A protractor is one tool that is used to measure an angle. Different shapes have different angle measurements. Angles are measured in degrees (º). A right angle measures 90º. An acute (uh-KYOOT) angle measures between 0º and 90º. An obtuse (uhb-TOOS) angle measures between 90º and 180º.

All the members of the landscaping team will use the plans as they work to complete our yard. The gardeners will know the measurements for the lawn and the gardens. The construction crew will know the measurements for the swimming pool and patio. Our designer will be able to work with the team by referring to the plans as he gets the job done.

Triangles and Quadrilaterals

A triangle has three vertices. That means it has three angles. The sum of the angles inside a triangle is always 180°.

A quadrilateral has four vertices and four angles. The sum of the angles inside a quadrilateral is always 360°.

Mosaics in Landscape Design

We have agreed on the detailed plans of our yard. We have chosen a lot of materials and elements to include in the design. Now we are ready to add a few interesting things. My parents talk to the landscape designer about including a **mosaic** (moh-ZEY-ik).

Mosaic Masterpiece

Mosaics are often functional in a garden. They are part of a wall or pathway. But mosaics can be art as well. These mosaics cover walls, pathways, and the garden of a home.

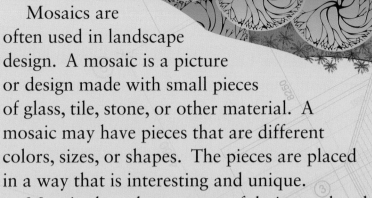

Mosaics are often used in landscape design. A mosaic is a picture or design made with small pieces of glass, tile, stone, or other material. A mosaic may have pieces that are different colors, sizes, or shapes. The pieces are placed in a way that is interesting and unique.

Mosaics have been a part of design and architecture for thousands of years! They can be found indoors or outdoors. We want to use a mosaic to add an artistic flair to our yard.

One thing I noticed about mosaics is that they can be simple or complex. They can cover a small area, like a planting box. They can also cover a large area, like an entire walkway, wall, or other surface. The beautiful thing that all mosaics share is the special way in which the materials are placed. When I look at a mosaic, I first notice the materials in it. Then I look closely at how the materials are arranged.

Swimming Pool Mosaics
Look closely at a swimming pool when you get a chance. You may notice that the tiles around the outside or inside of the pool are arranged in a mosaic style.

Our designer helps us decide on a few places to use this style in our own yard. We choose to create a small mosaic tabletop to use on our patio. We also cover a small wall in our garden with a glass mosaic design. These two things add an interesting look to our backyard.

LET'S EXPLORE MATH

Look at the mosaic design below.

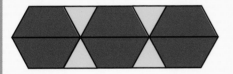

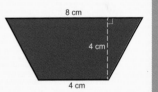

a. The yellow stone is an equilateral triangle. What is its perimeter?

b. What is the area of the triangular stone?

c. The perimeter of the trapezoidal stone is 20 cm. What are the lengths of the unlabeled sides?

d. Find the area of the trapezoidal stone.

A New Yard

Wow, it sure has been a lot of fun to design our yard! My family was able to contribute a lot of our own ideas to the plan. Our landscape designer and his team were able to create the yard that we all have been dreaming about for years.

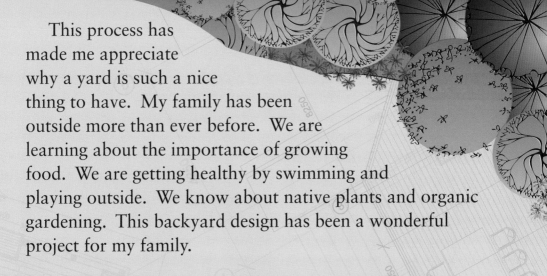

This process has made me appreciate why a yard is such a nice thing to have. My family has been outside more than ever before. We are learning about the importance of growing food. We are getting healthy by swimming and playing outside. We know about native plants and organic gardening. This backyard design has been a wonderful project for my family.

Building a Tree House

Jeff and Maria are working on a big project in their backyard. They are building a tree house with their father. Their father has helped them sketch a design to show how they want the finished product to look.

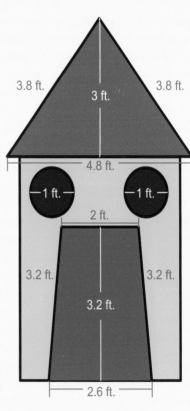

Solve It!

a. Find the perimeter and area of the door, the front of the roof, and each window of the tree house. Round your answers to the nearest hundredth.

b. What other measurements would be helpful for Jeff and Maria to know before they start building? Why?

Use the steps below to help you find the solutions.

Step 1: Find the perimeter and area of the door. Add all the sides together to find the perimeter. Use the formula for the area of a trapezoid: $A = \frac{1}{2}(b_1 + b_2)h$.

Step 2: Find the perimeter and area of the roof. Add all the sides together to find the perimeter. Use the formula for the area of a triangle: $A = \frac{1}{2}bh$.

Step 3: Find the circumference and area of one window. Use the formula for the circumference of a circle: $C = \pi d$ or $C = 2\pi r$. Use the formula for the area of a circle: $A = \pi r^2$.

Glossary

angles—figures formed by two rays that share an endpoint

area—the surface a flat object or region covers, measured in square units

border—to form a line along the edge of something

circumference—the distance around a circle

climate—the average weather in a region over a period of years

contrast—a difference, as compared with something else

diameter—the distance across a circle through the center

formula—a general mathematical rule represented in symbols, numbers, or letters, often in the form of an equation

gazebo—a circular building that is slightly elevated and usually found in parks or outdoor places

irrational number—a number that cannot be expressed exactly as a ratio of two integers

irregular—not even or symmetrical

mosaic—a picture or design made with small pieces of material

patio—a paved outdoor area, often used for outdoor dining

perimeter—the distance around the outside of an object or region

perpendicular—forming a right angle

polygon—a two-dimensional shape with three or more straight sides

protractor—an instrument used to measure and draw angles

radius—the distance from the center of a circle to any point on the circle

rays—parts of lines that begin at a point and extend indefinitely in one direction from the starting point

scale—a ratio representing the size of an illustration or reproduction in relation to the object it represents

trapezoid—a polygon that has exactly one pair of parallel sides, called bases

unique—being the only one of its kind

vertex—a point at which two rays, lines, or line segments meet to form an angle

Index

Let's Explore Math

Page 9:

perimeter: 455 ft.

area: 10,216.35 ft.^{2}

Page 10:

30.6 in.

Page 13:

a. 15.07 m; Answers will vary but may include: You may need to know the circumference of a circle to calculate the number of plants to buy to border a gazebo.

b. 18.09 m^2; Answers will vary but may include: You may need to know the area of a circle to calculate the amount of rocks needed to fill the inside of a circular rock garden.

Page 15:

a. perimeter: 24 in.; area: 27.6 in.^{2}

b. The perimeter of a triangle is the sum of its three sides, and the height is not a side of this triangle.

Page 17:

a. 20 m^2

b. 135 m^2

c. 155 m^2

Page 25:

a. 12 cm

b. 7 cm^2

c. 4 cm

d. 24 cm^2

Problem-Solving Activity

a. door—perimeter: 11 ft., area: 7.36 ft.^{2}; roof—perimeter: 12.4 ft., area: 7.2 ft.^{2}; window—circumference: 3.14 ft., area: 0.79 ft.^{2}

b. Answers will vary, but may include the height of the tree house from the ground (since they will need to build steps to get up to it), the dimensions of the floor (for buying materials), or how high the windows will be from the floor and how far they will be from the vertices (to know exactly where to cut the openings for them).